T0063909

THE EFFECTS OF CYBERCRIME IN THE U.S. AND ABROAD

Randall Knight, B.S., L.L.B, L.L.M.

authorHOUSE®

AuthorHouse™
1663 Liberty Drive
Bloomington, IN 47403
www.authorhouse.com
Phone: 1-800-839-8640

Published by AuthorHouse 11/052014

ISBN: 978-1-4969-4991-2 (sc)
ISBN: 978-1-4969-4990-5 (e)

Library of Congress Control Number: 2014919184

This book is being published in the memory of my mother Frances Nellie Morris Knight and my lovely daughter Niara Renee Knight.

CONTENTS

INTRODUCTION

In today's society computer technology has made it possible to communicate electronically in almost every aspect of life. The speed and efficiency of communicating electronically is overwhelming. Computers are used to store confidential data of social, economical, political and personal nature. Computer cybercrime refers to any crime that involves a computer and a network, where computers may or may not have played an instrumental part in the commission of the crime. Cybercrime activities include criminal offenses such as illegal downloading music files, stealing millions of dollars from on-line accounts. It also includes non-monetary offenses, such as creating and distributing computer viruses or posting confidential business information on the internet[1]. One of the most popular cybercrime activities that is posed in today's society is identity theft, which is the stealing of personal information such as passwords, phone numbers, addresses, credit card number and bank account information, etc. The cybercriminal gains access to this information in numerous ways. Once this information is

---

[1] Cybercrime http://www.techterms.com/definitions/cybercrime (last visited on June 6, 2011)

obtained the fraudulent process begins. This raises concerns of privacy invasion and the laws that protect them.

Another form of computer crime is referred to as Net crime[2]. Defined as criminal exploitation of the internet, it includes such crime as computer hacking, copyright infringement, child pornography, child grooming, etc. Net crime criminals; have the ability to engage in activities that include espionage, financial theft and cyber warfare. This raises concerns domestically and internationally. The U.S. Department of Defense reports that cyberspace has become a national-level concern. In 2007, an attack on Estonia's infrastructure was alleged to be done by Russian hackers. In 2008 Russian hackers conducted cyber attacks against the country of Georgia. There are literally thousands of cybercrimes that are committed, but few get caught and prosecuted. To solve this issue prevention and prosecution of offenders should be enforced to the fullest extent of the law.

Due to the global aspect of the internet and computer based commerce/communication, enforcement and prosecution is feasible undermined by the applicable laws which are based upon geographical boundaries. There is a need for global awareness for all countries involved in cybercrime offenses. Legislative laws should be amended and applied appropriately.

---

[2] http://www.ed.wikipedia.org/wiki/cybercrime (last visted on June 6, 2011)

I. History of Cybercrime

The birth of Electronic Technology dates back as far to 1876, when Alexander Graham Bell invented the telephone, which was used to communicate electronically. The first cybercrime was said to be committed in 1878. During the growth of his company Alexander Graham Bell used teenage boys to connect calls, provide information to customers using the service. Upon the publication of a book called The Hacker Crackdown[3]. They fired the teenage boy and replaced them with young women, who were deemed to respectable[4].

The birth of the Modern Internet was during the 1960's. It was known as ARPANET[5]., (Advanced Research Project of Agency). It was operated by the Department of Defense for defense purposes. It was the first widespread network of computer, packet switches, it began in 1969. It was linked to the Department of Defense, and several Universities such as University of California, Los Angeles, Stanford Research center, University of California at Santa Barbara and the University of Utah. In 1971 it was expanded to

---

[3] Bruc Sterling, The Hacker Crackdown: Law and Disorder on the Electronic Frontier. New York: Bantam 1992.

[4] Gina De Angelis, <u>Cybercrime</u> (1999) Chap 1, "the boys were openly rude to customers....saucing off, uttering facetious remarks, and generally giving lip....And worst of all, the played clever tricks with the switchboard plugs: disconnecting calls, crossing lines so that customers found themselves talking to strangers, and so forth. This combination of power, technical mastery, and effective anonymity seemed to act like catnip on teenage boys

[5] Cybersecurity & Cybercrime http://<u>www.oppapers.com/essays/</u> <u>Birth.Cyberlaw</u>. (last viewed on June 6, 2011

include additional universities and governmental agencies such as The National Aeronautics (NASA). The object was to create a network to be used to exchange information electronically. In 1973 other countries and other networks were capable of connecting with ARPANET. These networks were compatible because of the universal communication language that existed at that time. It was known as NCP, or Network Control Protocol. Today technology it is know as Transmission Control Protocol,

Internet Protocol, or TCP/IP. By 1986, the internet accessibility was available to anyone who owned a computer. The National Science Foundation Network (NSFNET) was the backbone of the internet[6]. In 1989 ARPANET was decommissioned and integrated into what is known today as the internet.[7]

The World Wide Web was created in 1993 by a software engineer and computer program Tim Berners-Lee. The World Wide Web was created to assist him in his work. Ultimately it soon became used by everyone. The Web was used to fulfill educational, technological and financial functions. With the stroke of a key the, world wide web enable transmission such as Electronic Mail and Chat rooms conversations with people instantly. The internet has become an important national infrastructure that is used world wide and in increasingly widespread and multicultural. It worldwide accessibility has created a multifaceted haven for criminals to blunder. Cybercrime committed in the

---

[6] *Id*

[7] *Id*

U.S. and internationally can be devastating personally to unsuspecting victims of the crime, computer networks, and U.S. infrastructures.

There are two types of computer cybercriminals who commit computer offense, commonly know as a computer hacker or a computer cracker. A computer hacker is defined as an individual or group of individuals who gain unauthorized access to a computer system, by hacking into it. The act of the computer hacker is generally not malicious. He/she is usually only interested in see if they can hack into a system, sometimes for fun, self fulfillment, entertainment or a challenge.

Crackers on the other hand activities are usually malicious and can damage to a computer network or system. This type of cybercriminal uses a code to gain unauthorized access to a computer network or system.[8]

In the landmark, case US v Mitnick[9]. Mitnick pleaded guilty to four counts of wire fraud, two counts of computer fraud and on count of illegally intercepting a wire communication. Mitnick admitted he broke into a number of computers systems and stole propriety software belonging to Motorola, Novell, Fujitsu, Sun Microsystems and other companies. Mitnick admitted using a number of tools to

---

[8]   J.A. Hitchcock, edited by Lorraine Page. Crimes & Misdemeanors: outmaneuvering web spammers, stalkers, and con artists 2nd ed. 2006.

[9]   US v Mitnick 525 U.S. 946; 119S. ct.370; 142 L. Ed. 2nd 306;(1998) 18 U.S.C § 1029(a)(3)

commit his crimes, including "social engineering," cloned cellular telephones, "sniffer" programs placed on victims' computer system and hacker software programs. He altered computer systems belonging to University of Southern California and used the computers to store misappropriated programs. He stole E-mail, monitored computer system and impersonated employees of companies such as Nokia Mobile Phone Ltd. Though, many of Mitnick's victims suffered millions of dollars in damages resulted from lost licensing fees, marketing delays, lost research and development, and repairs made to compromise computer system, Judge Pfaelzer orderd Mitnick to pay a total of $4,125.

A. Information Age

The internet is international, it is linked to computer network with a touch of a key stoke. This in essence erases the international boundaries that exist in other aspect of life. There are not boundaries in cyberspace. Basically anyone with a computer can access the internet and commit a computer crime. Cyberspace is where an enormous amount of electronic data exists for exchange. The use of the internet is based on trust and good conduct. Unfortunately there are those who disagree and use the internet for criminal activities. With the commission of thousand of different types of cybercrime offenses, the need for rule and order is necessary. Cybercrime is the cause and effect of what know today as cyber law.

B. White collar crime considerations

Cybercrime is considered to be a white-collar crime[10]., as opposed to blue-collar workers. Who are usually unskilled or semi-skilled worker. White collar crimes are typically committed by professional who have the ability and access to commit such crimes as embezzlement, imposture, and forgery[11]. The term white-collar criminal is view today as to simply mean, a non-violent or economic crime. White –collar crime associate with most business include business fraud, committed through peer to peer networks. Business cybercrimes can be committed by unauthorized access, computer hacking or trespassing. Malicious code attacks and malware attack can also be considered a white-collar act. Some white-collar crimes, which target business or industry infrastructures or telecommunication networks may lead to national security issues, and are considered a higher level of cybercrime. Other white-collar crimes are financial frauds, telecom frauds, fraudulent electronic transfer and bank fraud. Most of the cybercrimes that are committed are simply derived from greed, pride and are based on dishonesty. They are committed without force

---

[10] Bruce Sterling. The Hacker Crackdown: Law and Disorder on the Electronic Frontier. New York: Bantam 1992.

[11] "2003 CSI/FBI Computer Crime and Security Survey" internet http://www.usdoj.gov/criminal/cybercrime/CSI_FBI.htm. (last visited on June 6, 2011) In a 2003 survey conducted by the CSI with the participation of the San Francisco Federal Bureau of Investigation's Computer Intrusion Squad. of the 530 respondents made up of U.S. corporations, government agencies, financial institutions, medical institutions and universities, 56% reported unauthorized use of their computer systems

and require a degree of planning. Technology continues to become more easily than it was during the birth of the internet era. Today, computer can be accessed by anyone who has a cellular hand held phone. The World Wide Web can be accessed remotely. Cybercrime criminal today have acquired a vast knowledge of skills to commit computer crime, than the earlier computer hackers of the 1980's[12].

C. Aspects of international cybercrime criminals

Cybercrime activities are a global matter, with no boundaries. In 2007 the EastWest Institute with cooperation from the United States led by General (ret.) James Jones challenged, senior Chinese and Russian leader to begin a process of promoting international cooperation to meet cyber challenges. Ultimately the international cooperation

---

[12] Top Management and Performance Challenges in the Department of Justice 2008, http://www.justice.gov/oig/challenges/2008/ (last viewed on June 6, 2011. In a FBI 2005 Computer Survey described as conservative its 67.2 billion estimate of total loss to U.S. businesses from computer attacks. The Computer Security Institute (CSI) 2007 Computer Crime and Security Survey reported that the average loss suffered by a more limited number of survey respondents more than doubled from $168,000 in 2006 to 345,000 in 2007. This indicates that the economic impact of cybercrime is significant and growing. Moreover computers and other information technology systems have become part of our critical infrastructure, making their protection central to national security.

includes 40 Countries[13]. In 2009 the EWI's Worldwide Security Initiative[14] came together. Its purpose is to work across the borders to have a rapid response to cyber security challenges by industrial, governmental and international organizations. The challenge was due to the concern of the ever evolving vulnerabilities of today's infrastructure. They stressed the growing concern posed by criminal and terrorist groups, and the risk of cyber warfare. The top cyber experts from five countries – China, the US, Russia, India and Norway were called to present their view of how to create and effective system of cyber deterrence[15]. The have Chinese government argues that there are three major obstacles in place when it comes to combating cybercrime threats.

1. A lack of social responsibility and security awareness[16]
2. Inadequate international cooperation[17]
3. The reluctance of states perception of cybercrime interest or on difference in law and politics.[18]

In a report titled Strengthening International cooperation and joining hands in fighting against transnation cybercrime[19].

---

[13] Tang Lan, Zhang Xin, Harry D. Raduege, Jr., Dmitry I. Griegoriev, Pavan Duggal, and Stein Schjolberg. Global Cyber Deterrence – Views from China, the U.S., Russia, India, and Norway. April 2010. http://www.ewi.info (accessed June 6, 2011)

[14] *Id.*

[15] *Id.*

[16] *Id.*

[17] *Id.*

[18] *Id.*

[19] http://www.China.org.cn/business- (last viewed on June 6, 2011)

The Ministry of Public Safety G u Jim introduced a brief summary of cybercrime in China. He states the main types of cybercrime in China include pornography, gambling, fraud, hacker's attacks, illegal sales of contraband and infringement of Intellectual Property. Legislatively cybercrime in China are comprised of two aspects:

1. Cases involving pornography, gambling, fraud, illegal sale of contraband, infringement of Intellectual Property. For these crime the laws and regulation of convictions are adopted in punishment.
2. Cases involving hackers attacks and sabatoge, convictions are adopted in criminal law.

In China nearly 200 government websites are attacked daily, more than 80% of the attacks originate from foreign countries. China solution to the internet cybercrime and acts of terrorism, is too cooperated with law enforcement internationally to promote a closer more effective enforcement against cross-border cybercrimes activities. There international cooperation in combating cybercrime has strengthened the mechanism of combating cybercrime. They have established bilateral police cooperation with 30 countries such as U.S. Britain, Germany etc. They have created the Cybercrime Technology Information Network, System (CTINS) with Japan, republic of Korea and other Asian Countries. The Chinese Government has actively participated in the International Criminal Police Organization. Chinese officials argue that the substantive and procedural laws in different countries make it difficult to prosecute internationally. The Chinese Government continues to argue that as long as there are differences and disagreements between countries about the definition of cybercrime, the cyber threat cannot be dealt with appropriately. The report continue to state that the Chinese recognizes that internet security is a global problem and the international cooperation is needed in order to crack down on cybercrime, however all nations must respect the laws of their lands, politics and cultural traditions.

At the 16th World Computer Congress in 2000, they proposed a plan to develop and "International Internet Convention". They also came down heavy on cyber attacks, network viruses, hacker intrusion, illegal remote control computes and other problems that were deemed harmful to the security of communication network. In conclusion Chinese government suggests that there is a need to establish a universal or relatively uniformed international substantive and procedural law in combating cybercrime.

The U.S. response, it views the threat cyber attacks as one of the most important national security challenges today. In December 2008, the Center for Strategic and International Studies Commission on Cyber security for the 44th Presidency it was noted that the United States lacks the national strategy to address cyber threats[20].

On May 29, 2009, President Obama announced a series of initiatives including the establishment of a Cyber security Coordinator at the White House. Howard Schmidt was

---

[20] *Id.*

appointed to the position. His job is to orchestrate and integrate a cyber security policy for the entire Federal Government[21]. The U.S. views on the problem of cyber security in the digital age. By focusing upon a "Cyber Triad" that will deter cyberspace attacks on our networks using weapons of mass destruction.

1. The first leg of the new Cyber Triad is resilience; we must build resilience into our information systems, so our adversaries cannot succeed in attacking our networks[22].

2. The next step is attribution. In order to deter attacks we need to improve our capability to find the source of the attack[23].

3. The last Cyber Triad is offensive capabilities. Our enemies must know that America possess and effective offensive and defensive capabilities[24].

US view cyber deterrence cannot be undertaken by government alone. "To protect our information networks against espionage, crime and attacks in cyberspace, we need unprecedented private-public partnership[25]. It is estimated that about 11% of computer worldwide 65 to 90 million PC are compromised, because they lack firewall and anti-virus software.

---

[21] *Id.*

[22] *Id.*

[23] *Id.*

[24] *Id.*

[25] *Id.*

Russian Government is aware of cyber security issues and they have been studying the problems and awareness of the existing threats in cyberspace. The Russian Federation, have been collaborating with the leading Russian Government in dealing with the disagreement of cyber security at bilateral and multilateral levels. They argue that a universal language must be created when discussing cyber security issues. Different countries attach different meaning to the term. The Russian Government believes that cyber security involves three areas: Criminal, Terrorist and Military. Each entity is capable of mounting cyber attacks. They argue that in order to safeguard the security at the national level, the identity of the actor must be identified. Whether a criminal group, terrorist group or military they all appear to be growing stringing stronger, they have the capacity to have an impact in cyberspace. As a result the Russian Government states they need to make up a system of international and regional cyber security needs, based upon the establishment of a universal and comprehensive international law that doesn't allow the military to use the Internet for political purposes[26]. The Russian believe to accomplish this task the following must be adhered to:

1. Create an international system of Internet governance, which would call for the transfer of such functions as managing the system of domain names and root servers to the International Telecommunication Union[27].

---

[26] *Id.*

[27] *Id.*

2. Adopt a universal international political-legal pact that condemns the use of the Internet for military-political purposes[28].

3. Create regional information security systems that include international legal norms and threat monitoring[29].

4. Form a friendly global and regional information space based on principles of trust with forums such as UNESCO, the G8, the Council of Europe, etc… in order to prevent dissemination of inaccurate and deliberately false socio-political information[30].

5. Legislatively establish a unified agency for investigating cybercrime in order to prevent the use of the internet by criminals and terrorist purposes[31].

The Russian Federation believes that "A system of international and regional cyber security needs to be based on the idea of establishing a universal and comprehensive regime of international law that does not allow the use of the Internet for military-political purposes"[32].

In India, they have been looking at a variety of ways to legislate and effective system of cyber deterrence. They are one of the few countries that have use cyber law as means to

---

[28] *Id.*

[29] *Id.*

[30] *Id.*

[31] *Id.*

[32] *Id.*

have effective cyber deterrence[33]. India cyber law is designed to promote commerce and cyber deterrence.

Some of the provisions of the India cyber law

1. Tampering with source code documents was made a crime punishable by up to three years in prison or a fine up to 200,000 rupees, or by both[34].
2. Hacking was made an offense that is similarly punishable with imprisonment of up to three years or a fine of up to 200,000 rupees, or by both[35].
3. The law prohibits the publishing and transmitting of obscene electronic information, or causing such information to be published or transmitted. This crime is punishable with up to five years in prison and with a fine of up to 100,000 rupees[36].
4. Misrepresentation of any material facts while obtaining any license to act as a Certifying Authority or procuring a digital signature certificate was made a crime. The publishing of false digital signature certificates for fraudulent or unlawful purposes is punishable by up to two years in prison or by a fine of up to 100,000 rupees, or by both[37].

---

[33] *Id.* In 1997 the General Assembly of the United Nations endorsed the Model Law on Electronics Commerce. Keeping the model in mind, India enacted the Technology Act 2000, becoming the fifth nation in the world to enact cyber law.

[34] *Id.*

[35] *Id.*

[36] *Id.*

[37] *Id.*

With the existence of the India cyber law it became apparent it wasn't sufficient enough. In 2008 the Indian government enacted the Information Technology (Amendment) Act 2008. Indian law now became focus upon cyber deterrence. It amendment to the act defined cyber security as "protecting information equipment, devices, computer, computer resource, communication device and information stored therein from unauthorized access, use disclosure, disruption, modification, or destruction. The new enacted act focused upon all aspects of cyber crime and cyber terrorism.

As Indian law created laws to combat cyber crimes, they were not alone. The private sector also contributed in the battle. The Federal Reserve Bank of India mandated all banks to follow internet guidelines aimed to enhance security and reduce cyber attacks.

In conclusion[38], the Indian government argues that there are obstacles in place, on the international level, which hinders the efforts of cyber enforcement. There is a level of distrust between governments, different legislative approaches with dealing with cyber crime in the different countries. There is a need for the countries to work together.

The Indian government recommends.

---

[38] *Id.* "All countries need to realize that the Internet and cyberspace are shared by all of us, and that we need to collaboration at the international level to counter the broad range of threats".

1. India needs to come up with a cohesive national plan on cyber security[39].

2. A lot of government and private money, time, and effort need to be allocated for cyber security[40].

3. A broader awareness campaign is needed for all the relevant stakeholders[41].

4. India needs to participate actively in all forms of international cooperation on cyber security to promote more unified policies in the face of cyber threats[42].

5. India needs to further strengthen its laws pertaining to cyber security and make them into a more effective deterrent[43].

6. India needs to ensure that its existing laws are effectively implemented and do not remain mere paper tigers[44].

Norway position on Cyber deterrence is to create a global United Nations Framework in and effort to establish a Cyberspace Treaty, that would define cybercrime and it acceptable and unacceptable cyber behavior. To deter cyber threat a global strategy needs to be developed. It is their position that a United Nations Cyberspace Treaty would set the platform for a common understanding of all aspects of cyber security amongst the countries involved, define

---

[39] *Id.*

[40] *Id.*

[41] *Id.*

[42] *Id.*

[43] *Id.*

[44] *Id.*

what types of behaviors would constitute cybercrime, cyber terrorism and other forms of illegal cyber activity. It would reduce the divide between developed and developing countries perception of cyber security. Another issued discussed within the realms of a United Nations Cyber Treaty, is what jurisdiction a cyber crime offense should be punishable under, international or national law.

Norway believes that the offense of a cyber crime is a serious one and should be punishable under International Law, via a Cyber Space Treaty.

In May 2007, the International Telecommunication University (ITU) instituted the Global Cybercrime Agenda to help coordinate the challenges of cybercrime[45]. The major threats and concerns a Cyberspace Treaty will have to take into consideration are as follows:

- A. Categorization of cybercrime and the misuse of information technology would need to be considered[46].
- B. Cyber attacks may include the use of botnets designed to destroy or seriously disrupt critical information infrastructure of a network[47].
- C. Recruitment and training on the Internet for the purposes of a terrorism attack of a network of vital

---

[45] *Id.* "Criminal conduct in Cyberspace is global by nature and requires global harmonization of cybercrime legislation as part of a Cyberspace Treaty".

[46] *Id.*

[47] *Id.*

importance to society should be punishable as criminal offense[48].

D. Botnets service providers enabling criminals to plan or launch a cyber attacks which would compromised a computer network[49].

E. Identity theft fraud is a major concern[50].

Norway also believes that criminal prosecution based on International Law needs and International Criminal Court to conduct the proceeding[51]. The court would investigate and prosecute the act, if the state to the Rome Statute and they are unable to prosecute a crime. The jurisdiction of the (ICC) is limited to States that are party to the Statute. In conclusion the Norway is very interested in pursuing cyber deterrence by recommending the United Nations International Law Commission establish a partnership with other Global organization in battling cybercrime.

---

[48] *Id.*

[49] *Id.*

[50] *Id.*

[51] *Id.* The international Criminal Court (ICC) was established in 1998 as the first ever permanent treaty based, fully independent international criminal court.

II. Types of Cybercrimes (topology) in the US/International regions and it implications.

A. Cyber terrorsim

Cyber terrorism is a cyber criminal activity in which the Internet is utilized to commit deliberate large scale disruption of computer networks[52]. Cyber terrorism can be defined as any computer crime which targets a computer network, property or lives. Cyber terrorism acts us tactics to cause fear and panic to the targets of victims. There activities range from hacking into computers, spreading viruses to obtain information illegally as well as destroying or damaging computer networks.

The National Conference of State Legislature defines cyber terrorism as "the use of information technology by terrorist groups and individuals to further their agenda. This can include use of information technology to organize and execute attacks against networks, computer systems and telecommunication infrastructure, or for exchanging information or making threat electronically. Examples are hacking into computer systems, introducing viruses to vulnerable networks, web site defacing, denial of service attacks, or terroristic threats made via electronic communication"[53].

---

[52] http://en.wikipedia.org/wiki/cyberterrorism (last visited on June 6, 2011

[53] National Conference of State Legislatures http://ncsl.org/programs/lis/cip.cyberterrorism.html (last visited on June 6, 2011)

B.   Cyber warfare

Cyber warfare is defined by Richard A Clarke[54], a government security expert, in book titled Cyber war (May 2010), as "action by a nation-state to penetrate another nations- computers or network for the purposes of causing damage or disruption"[55].

In 2009, President Barack Obama stated "the American's digital infrastructure is a strategic National Asset"[56]. He then instituted a program (USCYBERCOM) to defend the American Military networks and attack other countries systems[57]. The department of Homeland Security is responsible for protecting government and Corporation infrastructures[58].

In an article by the Lipman Report dated 10/15/10, warns that the American cyber security defense has fallen behind the technological advances. There is a major concern of the types of destructive attacks that have already occurred.

---

[54]   Clarke, Richard. A Cyber War. Harper Collins (2010) (accessed June 6, 2011)

[55]   http://en.wikipedia.org.wiki.cyber warfare. (last visited on June 6, 2011)

[56]   *Id.*

[57]   *Id.* U.S. Cyber Command (USCYBERCOM) headed by General Keith B. Alexander. Director of National Security Agency (NSA).

[58]   *Id.*

U.S. v Robert Tappan[59] Morris; released a computer worm which caused damage to computer at various educational and military sites to cease functioning.

In 2009 a series of cyber attacks against government websites in US and other countries were effective in shutting down sites for several hours. It is believed that these successful attacks can grow into to future attacks on U.S. infrastructure, power generators or air traffic control systems. Concerns were address by Defense Secretary Robert Gates[60].

C. Cyber Stalking

A Cyber stalking acts is defined as threatening behavior or unwanted advances toward another by using the internet and other electronic communication tool, to harass annoy or cause alarm to another person. The technical advances in today society make it relatively easy for anyone to access a computer system and use it for criminal actions. Most cyber stalker access chat rooms, message boards, discussion forums and email accounts, to get victims. The stalking act is usually committed by sending threatening or obscene

---

[59] US v Robert Tappan Morris 928 F-20 504 1991 – US. App Lexis. 3682 Computer Fraud and Abuse Act of 1986 18 U.S.C. § 1030(a)(5)

[60] "There is no form of military combat more irregular than an electronic attack, fast and cheap, it can be carried out anonymously, allowing for plausible deniability and the lack of a return address, and can disrupt or deny critical services precisely at the moment of peril".
http://www.guardsmark.com//library/computer_security. asp? (last visited on June 6, 2011)

material via email, line chat, on-line verbal abuse, electronic viruses and electronic identity theft. The Cyber stalking activity is motivated by the desire to exert control over another individual. The majority of cyber stalkers are men and the majority of victims are women[61]. However some of the reported cases have been know to be cases against men being stalked by women and same sex stalking. Some cases of cyber stalking are committed by complete strangers. The enormous amount of personal date information on the internet ie, social network, the acts of cyber stalking can be easily committed. The internet and other forms of technology can be used to repeatedly send threatening or harassing messages with the stroke to a computer key. Cyber stalking can also be committed off-line, in which a person may experience abusive phone calls, vandalism, obscene mail, trespassing and physical assault.

The effects of cyber stalking can be traumatic to it victims, they can experience psychological trauma, physical and emotional problem which includes:

1. Eating and sleeping pattern change
2. Nightmares
3. Hyper vigilance
4. Anxiety
5. Helplessness
6. Fear of safety
7. Shock and disbelief

---

[61] http://www.ncvc.org/ncvc/main. aspx? (last visited on June 6, 2011)

Cyber stalking victims can take various steps to prevent and protect cyber stalking.

A. If you're receiving unwanted contact, make it clear to the sender that you do not want to be contacted.
B. Save all information received for evidence
C. Block or filter messages from the harasser
D. Consider changing e-mail addresses, ISP provider, home phone number, and use protective software.
E. Advise your ISP provider for their assistance in helping you protect yourself against a cyber stalker.
F. Contact the local Police Department and inform them of the situation.

Victims of cyber stalking can also seek help from support groups, family members and victim service professionals.

D. Spam

Spam[62] also know as junk email is usually in the for of an email advertisement, sent unsolicited[63] to email inboxes, mail list, newsgroups in bulk amounts, sent as a large of a collection of identical messages. Spam can also be used

---

[62] Net Crimes & Misdemeanors – Outmaneuvering web spammers, stalkers, and con artist. J/A Hitchcock: 2nd Ed. "unsolicited electronic junk mail, usually advertisement or offers, and, more often than not, unwanted by the receiver; sometimes used as revenge tatic by pretending to be someone, then spamming messages to hundreds, sometimes thousands of people".

[63] http://www.Spanhaus.org/definition.html - "meaning that the recipient has not granted verifiable permission for the message to be sent.

to spread computer viruses, Trojans horses and malicious software. In 2011, it is estimated that 7 trillion messages have been sent via spam. Cisco system reported in 2009 a list of the origin of spam countries[64].

Rank	Country	Spam messages per year (in trillions)
1	Brazil	7.7
2	United States	6.6
3	India	3.6
4	South Korea	3.1
5	Turkey	2.6
6	Vietnam	2.5
7	China	2.4
8	Poland	2.4
9	Russia	2.3
10	Argentina	1.5

The problem of spamming is the subject of legislation in some jurisdictions. In 2007 California legislatures found that the spam emailing messages has cost the U.S. more than 13 billion dollars in lost, the lost includes such factors as lost of productivity, purchasing of additional equipment, software, and manpower needed to challenge the intrusion of spam messaging[65].

---

[64] http://en.wikipedia.org/wiki/Spam_(electronic)

[65] *Id.*

On 5/31/07 a man know to and named by the authorities as the Seattle Spammer[66], was charged with 35 criminal count, including mail fraud, wire fraud, email fraud, aggravated identity theft and money laundering. Prosecutes accused him of using millions of "zombie" computers to distribute spam.

E. On-line Hoax

Hoaxes are messages and post sent by email to unsolicited recipients, in an effort to convince that they are, or will, receive items for no fee, or a virus warning. Some other forms of hoaxes are messages asking the recipient to forward the email to 10 other friend with the reward of good luck, good health or success, to follow. The common on-line hoax usually request some sort of medical condition has occurred and they are asking for your help in raising money to pay for medical bills. They usually ask for a contribution of $1.00 dollar, and then suggest that you forward the email to other people for their response to the email request. These types of hoax are known as a chain letter.

Below is a list of the Top 10 worst internet hoaxes and spam in US history.[67]

1. Next Time, Just Say "I Don't Know". Urgent email requests

---

[66] U.S. v Soloway No. CR07-187 MJP US District Ct. for Western District of Washington, 2007 US Dist Lexis 66641- 9/21/07 U.S.C. § 1028A (a)(1)(7) - 18 U.S.C.§ 1037(a)(2)(3)(b)(1) (A) -18U.S.C. § 1341 18 U.S.C. § 1956(a)(1) (A)(1)

[67] http://archives.cnn.com/2001/TECH/internet/12/24/internet. hoaxes.idg (last visited on June 6, 2011)

2. Last Photo From the World Trade Center Deck. A photo posted on the Web of a tourist posing of the observation deck minute before the airline crashed into it.

3. Deodorant Endangers Your Health. A convincing sounding message from a woman who attended a health seminar, warned that deodorant can cause breast cancer.

4. The $250 Cookie Recipe. Someone ate a cookie at a restaurant and was charged $250 instead of $2.50.

5. Save Big Bird. A email hoax professing that PBS needed support to keep running.

6. Money Nonsense in Nigeria. A email message which states the Nigerian government wants to deposit millions of dollars into your account. All that needed is your name and bank account information.

7. Dial 809 for trouble. A message requesting to call a number in the 809 area code (a Caribbean prefix) to clear up and outstanding account. It charged $25 a minute to access.

8. Bill Gates Reaches Out to you. A message stating the Bill Gates wants to give you Money.

9. Help a Sick Child. A message requesting that a child is dying of cancer and to forward the email to others. In return the America Cancer Society will donate money.

10. Let the Good Times Roll. A phony bulletin, email message which ask recipients not to read or download any files with the name Good Times.

In conclusion if an email message looks suspicious most likely it's a hoax or a scam.

F.   Internet Shopping

Shopping on the Internet is considered safe as long as you use your credit card when making an on-line purchase[68]. A credit card transaction purchase is a form of protection for the purchaser against scams or merchant arrogance. Credit card purchases are able to notify their bank and dispute the item in question. If the purchase is made by check or money order, there is little of no recourse of action that a consumer can take. MasterCard International and the National Consumer's League suggest ways to make an on-line purchase successful[69].

1. Privacy protection
2. Information about the offer
3. Information about the seller
4. Deliver date
5. Security
6. Guard personal records
7. The seller reputation
8. Consider Tax & Shipping cost
9. Insurance
10. Keep records

When shopping on line it is suggested that you shop on website that are secured with Secured Socket Layer (SSL).

---

[68] J/A Hitchcock, edited Lorraine Page, Net Crime & Misdemeanors: outmaneuvering web spammers, stalkers, and con artist "The most common mistake online shopper make is not using a credit card" 2nd ed 2006

[69] *Id.*

A website with (SSL) scrambles your personal information which allow for a safe transmission of the transaction[70].

G. Auction Fraud

Internet fraud is steadily growing worldwide. With the boom and ease of online shopping has spawned auction fraud and scams. In 2002, 51,000 cases of fraud was reported[71]. In 2006, the number of fraud complete almost doubled to 97,000.[72] Auction fraud occurs when the seller offers an item on line for sale, but the item is not genuine. It usually in the form of a forged autograph or memorabilia, videos, music, pirated software, etc... with auction bidding done usually with, business-to-consumer or consumer-to-consumer, transaction. Once the auction is over, the seller deals directly with the buyer in obtaining payment for the item. Auction fraud is usually conducted be email correspondence or through Ebay, with payment being made through an electric online payment service such as Paypal, types of Internet auction fraud usually involves the following:

1. Non delivery of the item, usually there is no item at all.
2. Misrepresentation by deceiving the buyer as true value of an item, usually done by listing false information when offering an item for sale.
3. Triangulation which involves the seller (perpetrator), the consumer and an online merchant.

---

[70] *Id.*

[71] http://www. crimecheck.com/background.check-news/ (last viewed on June 6, 2011

[72] *Id.*

4. Fee Stacking is when the seller adds hidden charges to an item occurring when the auction ends. Usually hidden in shipping and postage fee's.

5. Black market goods for sale on Internet auction sites

6. Multiple bidding to buy and item at a lower price. Occurs when 1 buyer uses multiple alias and bids high on an item to escalate the price of the item.

7. Shill bidding is intentional fake bidding to drive up the price of their own item for sale.

In 2008 the top Cybercrime complaint received by Internet Crime Complaint Center, which received 70,000 complaints during the year of 2007 is as follows[73].

2008 Top 10 Complaint Categories
(Percent of Total Internet Crime Complaints Received)

Category	Percent
Non-delivery	32.9%
Auction Fraud	25.5%
Credit/Debit Card Fraud	9.0%
Confidence Fraud	7.9%
Computer Fraud	6.2%
Check Fraud	5.4%
Nigerian Letter Fraud	2.8%
Identity Theft	2.5%
Financial Institutions Fraud	2.2%
Threat	1.9%

Source: IC3

---

[73] http/:www.fbi.gov/news/stories/2009/june/auctionfraud (accessed on June 6, 2011)

H. Phishing Scam[74]

1. Nigerian Hoax is a scam usually sent by email or a fax and with the advancement of technology, it is sent via email. It is also know as the "419 scam", "advance fee scam," and the "Spanish prisoner con." Originating in Nigeria, it is a scam with the intent get money from unsuspecting people who fall for it. Listed below are a few examples of people who fell for the scam:

"A financial manager from Austria took 1 million from his clients because he really believed he was going to make more than 60 times the amount if he followed the instructions of Reverend Sam Kukah, the chairman of Nigeria's Presidential Payment Debt Reconciliation Committee, who needed to transfer a huge sum of money offshore. This was an urgent transaction! And the financial manager believed him. He was arrested (not the Nigerian, who disappeared with million bucks) and could spend up to 10 years in jail for deceiving his clients and stealing their money"[75]

"A businessman in the United Kingdom lost 200,000 and his business. He received an email from a man calling himself Vincent who claimed he had $12 million he wanted to move from South Africa to the U.K. and asked if he the businessman would help. He said he would and

---

[74] *Id.* A play on the word "fishing," when scammer try to get you to reply or take them up on an offer to make money, or they claim your account needs to be verified by reconfirming everything from you user ID and password, to credit, banking, and other information.

[75] *Id.*

when "promises" arose, he was asked to invest $7,000 in an offshore account to get the ball rolling. The ball didn't stop until he was out of $200,000. His business failed as a result of the losses.

An elderly man in Florida lost his entire life saving for over $300,000 to a Nigerian scam and he was still having a hard time believing they scammed him".

People seem to fall for these types of scams because they are trustworthy of the internet; they are sometime amazed at the wealth they would be gaining if it wasn't a scam[76].

Another Phishing scam is purported by attempted to fraudulently using Paypal, an online payment service used to transfer money electronically. Through phishing, a scam artist will set up a phony Paypal website, the scam artist then contacts retailers via email that use the service and request they confirmation of confidential account information such as passwords[77]

I.   Identity Theft

Identity theft occurs when someone steals your identity, impersonates you and uses your good name to do a variety of transactions. The imposter illegally obtains personal data

---

[76] *Id.*

[77] Steve Weisman, 50 ways to Protect your identity and credit card. "warning Paypal never ask for personal financial information by way of email and never refers to previous transactions through email. If you get such an email, do not reply to it, but inform Paypal by telephone directly of the email message received." 2005

and uses the date to impersonate the identity of someone. The personal data includes the victim's social security number, date of birth, address, cell phone number, and credit card information to illegally take out loans, make credit card purchases, ordering items. Some impersonators even commit crimes using the identity of the unsuspecting victims. Identity theft done on line is easily obtained by a Web-savvy thief. The Federal Trade Commission identifies some of the ways that an identity thief criminal can get personal information[78]:

1. They steal wallets and purses containing your identity and credit/bank card information.
2. They steal you mail, including your bank and credit card statements, pre-approved credit offers, telephone calling cards and tax information.
3. They complete a "change of address form" to deliver your mail to another location.
4. They rummage through your trash, or the trash of businesses, for personal data in a practice know as "dumpster diving."
5. They fraudulently obtain your credit report buy posing as a landlord, employer, or someone else who may have a legitimate need and a legal right to the information.
6. They get you business or personal information records at work.
7. They find personal information in your home.

---

[78] Robert J. Hammond Jr. Identity theft: how to protect your most valuable asset, 2003

8. They use personal information you share on the Internet.

9. They buy your personal information from "inside" sources. Example and identity thief may pay a store employee for information about your personal information that appears in their database.

In many cases the victim is unaware that their identity was compromised until they start receiving phone calls and mail from collection agencies. U.S. v Mantovani et al.[79] a 62- count indictment, returned by a federal grand jury in Newark, N.J., alleged that 19 individuals from across the United States and in several foreign countries conspired with others to operate "Shadow crew" a website with approximately 4,000 members that was dedicated to facilitating malicious computer hacking and the dissemination of stolen credit cards, debit cards and bank accounts numbers and counterfeit identification documents, such as driver's licenses, passports and Social Security cards.

One of the worst case scenarios is when the victims identity is used in the commission of a crime and the victims is face with criminal charges derived from the imposter[80].

---

[79] U.S. v Mantovani et al Date Filed 10/26/2004, 18U.S.C. § 371 &2; 18 U.S.C. § 1028(a)(2); 18 U.S.C. § 1029(a)(1); 18 U.S.C.§ 1029(a)(2); and 18 U.S.C. § 1029(a)(6)(A)

[80] Id.

"Any activity in which identity information is shared or made available to other creates an opportunity for identity theft[81]".

Victims of identity are face with the enormous task of repairing their good name and credit. In order to repair some of the damage which is done by the imposter, most likely the victim has to submit an affidavit to the credit attesting the debt incur is the result of identity theft. Identity theft defrauds banks and cost million of dollars a year. It also endangers economic security and consumers.

J.   Child Pornography & Exploitation

Child pornography is defined under Federal Law 18 U.S.C.S § 2256) as any visual depiction, including any photograph, film, video, picture, or computer or computer generated image or picture, whether made or produced by electronic, mechanical, or other means, of sexually explicit conduct where

1.   the production of the visual depiction involves the use of a minor engaging in sexually explicit conduct; or
2.   the visual depiction is a digital image, computer image, or computer-generated image that is, or is indistinguishable from, that of a minor engaging in sexually explicit conduct; or

---

[81]   Sean B. Hoar, US department of Justice, Executive Office for United States Attorneys. ("Identity theft: The Crime of the Millennium.") USA Bulletin, March 2001, Vol. 49, No. 2. p. 1.

3. the visual depiction has been created, adapted, or modified to appear that an identifiable minor is engaging in sexually explicit conduct

Child pornography and exploitation of children is a Federal crime punishable by Federal laws in all 50 States & District of Columbia. Any person who knowingly possess, manufactures of distribute or access images of minor children will be prosecuted under Federal and State laws U.S. Alberston[82]. Child pornography image can be found to exist on print media, videotape, film, CD-ROM, or DVD. It is know to be accesses on the internet, newsgroups, chat rooms, instant messaging services, email, website and peer to peer technology.

K. Intellectual Property

The concept of Intellectual Property is to protect the rights of the creators in the field of industrial, scientific, and artistic productions and creations. The principles of Intellectual

---

[82] US v Albertson, 2011 U.S. App. Lexis 9106 §2252(a)(2)(B) Any person who knowingly receives, or distributes, any visual depiction using any means or facility of interstate or foreign commerce or that has been mailed, or has been shipped or transported in or affecting interstate or foreign commerce, or which contains material which have been mailed or so shipped or transported, by any means including by computer, or knowingly reproduces any visual depiction for distribution using any means or facility of interstate of foreign commerce or in or affecting interstate

Property dates back to the late 20th century[83] before it became the commonplace in the U.S. The law that governs Intellectual Property is in place to safe guard the creators of intellectual good and services. Under Intellectual laws the owners are granted certain exclusive rights to a variety of intangible assets such as, musical, literary, and artistic work; discoveries and invention; and works, phrases, symbols and designs.

Types of Intellectual Property include:[84]

A. Copyrights
B. Trademarks
C. Patents
D. Industrial design rights
E. Trade secrets.

These exclusive rights given to the creators allows them to benefit monetarily is their product is used or access. U.S. v Montejano[85], who conspired to commit copyright infringement, by reproducing and distributing, copyrighted music on the internet. The access of music on the internet is overwhelming. He was member and leader of an Internet music release group know as "Old School Classic" or "OSC", which specialized in distributing music on internet.

---

[83] http://www.en.Wikipedia.org/wiki/intellectual property(last viewed on June 6, 2011)

[84] *Id.*

[85] U.S. v Montejano cr 09-1330(A) U.S. Central Distict of California May 2, 2011.

In another case trade secrets were access and stolen. U.S. v Aleynikov[86], a former Goldman Sachs computer programmer stole a proprietary computer code, violating a confidentiality agreement.

III. Who are the victims.

A. Consumers

Many consumers are reluctant to make purchases on the internet in fear that their personal information will be fraudulently misused. Consumers have suffered identity theft, lost jobs, suffered loss of income, etc, all because their personal private information was inappropriately used or accessed inappropriately. In the first 3 months of 2011, 2,884,931 people have had their identity stolen; there is a 65% chance of being a target for identity thief by a cybercriminal[87]. U.S. v Ardolf[88], hacked into his neighbor computer impersonated him and sent threatening messages to kill the Vice-President and a U.S. senator from Minnesota. He was arrested for aggravated identity thief.

---

[86] U.S. v Alenikov 1:10 cr -00096 U.S. Southern District of New York, March 18, 2011

[87] http://www.investmentu.com/video/oxf (last viewed on June 6, 2011)

[88] U.S. V Ardolf, Minnesota, cr- 10-159 (DWF) 18 U.S.C. §1028(A) 18 U.S.C. § 871(A)

The U.S. Federal Commission[89] functions, is to educate consumers and business about the importance of personal information privacy, accuracy of personal information when using the internet.

B. Business Owners

Cybercrime committed by the use of the internet can affect businesses in more than one way. Financially is the main problem posed by the cyber act. Once the financial integrity of a business is compromised[90] the main effect of it is loss of revenue. Once a Cybercriminal accesses sensitive financial information, they can make withdrawal, transfer funds, wire money, etc. Another factor directly related to the financial integrity of a business, is once an e-commerce website is attacked and compromised, income is automatically lost until the site is operable again. The consequences of repairing a website by I.T. specialist can be time consuming and costly. The company reputation can also be damaged, public trust is compromised. The cybercrime act can also be harmful to sensitive company record (credit card account information and other personal information), subjecting customers to identity thief possibilities. Once a cyber breach is committed businesses have a duty to protect their database, and increase the efforts in protecting their databases.

The problems of cybercrime activity are widespread and can affect the infrastructure of some business. Inventory

---

[89] http://www.ftc.gov (last viewed on June 6, 2011)

[90] http://www. ehow.com/print/about (last viewed on June 6, 2011

Locator Service LLC v Partsbase Inc[91], the defendant gained unauthorized access to the plaintiff database and obtained and used improper information to solicit the plaintiff's customers. According to the Federal Bureau of Investigation (F.B.I) 2004 Internet Fraud Report, reports that the agency received 207,449 complaints during that year[92]. This statistic also showed an increased of 125,509 reported filed cases from the previous year. The FBI fraud report of 2004, also reported that on their website, which was set-up to deter cybercrime more than 150 investigations were conducted in reference to cybercrime. It resulted in that 870,000 victims lost more than $210 million dollars during that year alone[93].

Department of Homeland Security published a guide to help business prevent and protect their computer databases[94].

Common Sense Guide to Cyber Security[95]

1. Use strong Passwords and Change them regularly
2. Look Out for E-Mail Attachments and Internet Download Modules

---

[91] Inventory Locator Service LLC v Partbase Inc 2005 U.S. District Lexis 46252 (W.D. Tenn. Oct 19, 2005

[92] http://www. Federal Bureau of Investigations and National White Collar Crime Report (4) (ED)(2005. Jan.) IC3 2004 Internet Fraud-Crime Report (4).

[93] http://www. fbi.gov/cybercinvest/Websnare.htm (last viewed on June 6, 2011)

[94] http://www.global datavault.com/blog/common sense guide to cyber security (last viewed on June 6, 2011)

[95] *Id.*

3. Install, Maintain, and Apply Anti-Virus Programs
4. Install and Use a Firewall
5. Remove Unused Software and User Accounts; Clean Out Everything on Replaced Replaced Equipment
6. Establish Physical Access Controls for all Computer Equipment
7. Create Backups for Important Files, Folders, and Software
8. Keep Current with Software Updates
9. Implement Network Security with Access Control
10. Limit Access to Sensitive and Confidential Data
11. Established and Follow a Security Financial Risk Management Plan; Maintain Adequate Insurance Coverage
12. Get Technical Expertise and Outside Help When You Need It

C. Government Effect

Cyber terrorist in today society are not only concerned with attacking and infiltrating business and government data bases the are now concentrated on stealing your life saving or retirement fund, which in turn damages our economy and infrastructure according to Matthew Carr[96], reports that the Pentagon Officials believe that sophisticated hackers can easily[97]. "Disable critical infrastructure in a major city, steal millions of dollar from banks all over the world, infiltrate defense systems, extort millions from public companies and

---

[96] Matthew Carr. Cyber Security Specialist The Oxford Club 4/2011 (www.innvestment.com/video/oxf.)

[97] *Id.*

even sabotage our weapon systems". He continues by stating "the government is grossly unprepared for cyber attacks. In a report by The Center for Strategic and International Studies report companies who run critical infrastructure systems such as electronic banking, electrical grids and oil supplies have already sustained cyber attack by organized groups. The concern of security threats and the intrusion posed on the U.S. Government Computer and Networks is a major concern of the U.S. Department. In 1996, after a hacker attacked AT & T Communications, the Justice Department launched a program to go after the hackers. They created the National Infrastructure Protect Center, to protect major U.S. Communication, Transportation and Technology infrastructures, against computer hackers.

U.S. v Tenebaum[98]. Ehud Tenebaum illegally accessed computer belonging to the Israeli and U.S. Government, as well as commercial and educational systems in the U.S. and elsewhere. A top U.S. Intelligence Official states[99], "the Chinese have already aggressively infiltrated the computer system of some U.S. banks and are operating inside U.S. electrical grids, mapping out our networks and presumably leaving behind malicious software that could be used to sabotage the system". The U.S. government has taken several steps in combating cyber terrorism and cyber warfare. There are bills being proposed to Congress to defeat the threat of protecting Cyberspace. On May 12, 2011 President Obama revealed legislative proposals requesting critical

---

[98] U.S. v Tenebaum cr-00747-ERK (3/18/98)The Dept. of Justice, FBI, U.S. Airforce Office of Special Investigations Service.

[99] *Id.*

infrastructure operators in private sectors, list their threats and vulnerabilities and then institute a plan on fixing the systems threats with a plan[100].

IV. Reducing the Risk of Cyber attacks on Computer Networks

A. History of Computer Viruses

The first P.C. Virus was created in 1986. It was called the "Brain Virus"[101], originating in Pakistan. It functioned to only affect boot records of the computer system. In 1981 another computer virus was invented; it was called Lehigh[102] it was created and discovered at Lehigh University. The virus attacks the memory resident files of a computer, infecting and attacking executable files. In 1998 the first written anti-virus program was written to detect and remove the Brain virus. There are many different types of virus program that affect computer systems or computer network in different ways, causing damage or compromising the security of a computer system. Trojan Horses are another type of virus, they are usually sent in the form of a joke program or software. Trojans provide a way to highjack and control a computer

---

[100] who is responsible for cyber security, http://www. National defense magazine.org/archive/2011/June/pages/ (last viewed June 6, 2011

[101] what is a computer virus. http://www. pcsecurityalert.com/ pcsecurityalert-articles.(last viewed on June 6, 2011

[102] *Id.*

system. U.S. v Garcia[103]. A former employee of Viewsonic Corporation hacked into the company's computer wiping out critical data, which in turn shut down the company's computer server that was central to their foreign operations. Trojan Horses main functions, is to cause data destruction and compromises the computers integrity by providing the mean for other computer to access it. A Worm virus is another type of virus that can infect a computer system by distributing copies of itself moving from one disk drive to another by using email to copy itself. It causes damage and compromises to security of a computer system or network. Malicious attacks and cyber activity targeting U.S. computers and networks are preventable. Malicious attacks against computer networks can be devastating. They are used to attack computer networks and systems by attaching a malicious code that exploits vulnerabilities in a computer system. It modifies or destroys critical data, allows unauthorized access, conceals or destroys information stored on a computer's hard drive or database and damaging the computer system.

Malware is another avenue that is used by Cybercriminals to attack a computer system. It is defined as a software virus used to destroy data, key logger, steal passwords.

Other type of virus are displayed on the following chart[104]

---

[103] U.S. v Garcia C.D. Cal, 2/23/04

[104] http://www.guard-privacy online security.com/computer virus definition.html(last viewed on June, 2011

TABLE 1. Computer Virus Definition... Types Of Viruses

Virus Type	What It Does	How Affects Our PC
Program or File Virus	Infects executables (other programs, with affixes such as EXE, BIN, COM, SYS)	Destroys or alters programs and data.
Boot sector Virus	Infects boot sectors on hard and floppy disks	Destroys or alters programs and data.
Multipartite Virus	A hybrid of a program and boot sector virus	Destroys or alters programs and data.
Macro Virus	Triggers on a command in Microsoft Office	Commonly affects Word & Excel
Stealth Virus	Uses various tactics to avoid detection.	Destroys or alters programs and data.
Polymorphic Virus	Uses encryption to foil detection, so that it appears differently in each infection.	Destroys or alters programs and data.

B. Protecting Computer Network against attacks

Anyone who uses a computer is vulnerable to a cyber attack if they don't have some sort of protection installed on their computer systems. Protection can be in the form of Firewall protection, which when activate on a computer system essentially blocks unwanted communication from unknown source to access your system. Another form of protection is Encryption, which is the process of transforming information to make it unreadable to anyone except those who have and interactive key code to access the data. Another technique used to protect the integrity and confidentiality of a message is a message authentication code or MAC. Digital signatures are another form of Cryptography. Password protection is another form of protecting a network; passwords are used to restrict the access of a network to the password holder. It protects the computer system from unwanted unauthorized access. An advanced network may require a systems specialist, who specializes in securing databases and network against intrusions. A computer hacker can havoc to a computer system, national critical infrastructure and business across the United States. Cyber security and protecting data and information on a computer system can be done by following the simple steps outline below[105]:

1. Use Anti-Virus software and keep it up to date.
2. Don't open email from unknown sources.
3. Use hard to guess passwords.
4. Protect your computer from Internet intruders by using firewalls.
5. Back up your computer date.
6. Regularly download security protection updates known as patches.
7. Check your security on a regular basis.
8. Make sure your co-workers know what to do if your computer system becomes infected.
9. Participated in National Cyber Security Awareness Month.

---

[105] http://www.ready-gov/business/protect/cybersecurity.html (last viewed June 6, 2011)

V. Cybercrime laws and Statutes

A. USA Patriot ACT

There are over 40 Federal Statutes that govern the prosecution of computer related crimes. The USA Patriot Act (H.R. 3162) Sec 814 is an Act signed into law by President George W. Bush on 10/26/01. The Act reduces the legal restrictions on search capabilities of telephone, e-mail communications, medical, financial and other records. It also eased restrictions on foreign intelligence gathered in the U.S., broadened the discretion of law enforcement and Immigration Officers for detaining and deportation of illegal immigrants suspected of terrorism.

The Act consists of ten titles. Sec 814 of the Act addresses the issues of cyber terrorism[106].

Section 814 Deterrence and Prevention of Cyber terrorism

Computer Fraud and abuse is a federal crime when it involves a federally protected computer, I.e., a federal computer, a computer used by financial institutions, or a computer used in interstate or foreign commerce, 18 U.S.C. 1030. Section 814 increases the penalty for intentionally damaging a protected computer from imprisonment for not more than 5 years to imprisonment for not more that 10 years. It also raises the penalty for either intentionally or recklessly damaging a protected compute after having previously been convicted of computer abuse from imprisonment for not more than 10 years imprisonment for not more than 20 years.

---

[106] Congressional Research Service * Library of Congress

In order to trigger criminal or civil liability for causing damage to a federally protected computer, the damage must fall into one of several categories. It must involve losses of $5000 or more, or adversely affect certain medical data, or cause a physical injury, or threaten public health or safety. Section 814 supplies a fifth category – damaging affecting a computer system used by or for the government for the administration of justice, national defense, or national security.

The Department also addresses the issues of Cyber terrorism through their Computer Crime and Intellectual Property Section, which is responsible for creating a comprehensive plan of action to combat cybercrime penetration, data thefts, and cyber attacks on critical information systems. They work with other government agency to investigated and prosecute computer crimes. CCIP[107] also enforces crime against Intellectual Property, which is one the supportive backbones of the economy. They are responsible for the national strategies in combating computer and intellectual property cases worldwide.

B. Gramm-Leach-Bliley Act

Under this Act, which was enacted in 1999 and signed into law by President Clinton, it contains provisions to protect consumers financial information collected from financial institutions from being disclosing personal information to others. The act contains provisions that pertain to protecting

---

[107] Computer Crime and Intellectual Property Section. http://www.cybercrime.gov (last viewed June 6, 2011

a consumer's personal information and privacy of non-public information, how it is collected and disclosed. The Act focuses upon three areas for discussion. Privacy of personal information compliance from financial institutions is mandatory, they are required to ensure security and confidentiality of customer's information and a policy must be in place to protect the information against any anticipated threats or hazards to the integrity of the information.

Personal information includes;

> Financial Privacy Rules[108] (Subtitle A: Disclosure of Nonpublic Personal Information Codified at 15 U.S.C.§§ 6801.

1. Requires financial institutions to provide each consumer with privacy notice explaining that the information collected from the consumer is stored, shared, how it is used and how it is protected. The rule also incorporated and opt-in, opt out clause

2. The Safeguard Rule[109] requires financial institution to develop a security plan describing how they plan to protect non-public information[110].

---

[108] Gramm-Leach-Bliley Act (15 U.S.C.§§6801-6809) Disclosure of Non-Public Information. http://www.gpo.gov

[109] *Id.*

[110] *Id.* Meaning personal identifiable financial information that is provided be a consumer to a financial institution; (2) resulting from any transaction with the consumer or any service performed for the consumer, or otherwise obtained by the financial institution.

3. Pretexing Protection[111] is protection of the consumer private information from being disclosed to unauthorized persons who impersonate the account holder, by phone, mail, e-mail or phishing by using phony website to illegally obtain personal information.

Section 521(a) of the Act prohibits the illegally obtaining information from a financial institution by means of misrepresentation or fraud. This practice is know as Pretext calling, in which an Identity theft seeks out consumer accounts information for defrauding purposes.

C. Children's Online Privacy Protection Act of 1998

The Children On line Privacy Act[112] is Act became effective on 4/21/00, its primary goal is to place parents in control of what information is being collected from children while they are on-line. It protects children under the age of 13, personal information from being disclosed without their

---

[111] *Id.*

[112] Children's Online Privacy Protection Act (COPPA), 15 U.S.C.§§ 6501-6508 1998. http://www.ftc.gov/privacy (last viewed on June 6, 2011)

permission or knowledge. The rule applies to operators of websites and online services[113].

The rule must:

1. Post clear and comprehensive privacy policy on their disclosing their information practices for children personal information[114].
2. Provide direct notice to parents and obtain verifiable parental consent, with limited exceptions, before collecting personal information from children[115]
3. Give parent the choice of consenting to the operators collection and internal use of child's information, but prohibiting the operator from disclosing that information to third parties[116]
4. Provide parents access to their child's personal information to review and /or have the information deleted[117]

---

[113] (A) means any person who operates a website located on the internet or online service and who collects or maintains personal information from or about the users or visitors to such website or online service, or on whose behalf such information is collected or maintained, where such website or online service is operated for commercial purposes, including any person offering products or services for sale through that website or online service involving commerce. http://www.ftc.gov/org/coppa (last viewed on June 6, 2011)

[114] *Id.*

[115] *Id.*

[116] *Id.*

[117] *Id.*

5. Give parent's the opportunity to prevent further use or online collection of a child personal information[118]
6. Maintain the confidentiality, security and integrity of information they collect from children[119]

The Federal Trade enforces the rules by monitoring the internet for compliance, law enforcement action are taken against violators of the Act.

D. Identification Theft and Assumption Deterrence Act

The Identification Theft and Assumption Deterrence Act was enacted in 1998. It criminalizes the act of taking another person's identity, such as identifying information, name, date of birth, social security numbers. Is also covers the fraud aspects of identification theft and the misuse of personal identifying information unlawfully used in documents, software or computer files. The concern of identification theft is of high importance in today's society. The Federal Trade Commission release a report in 2007 reports that 8.3 million Americans adult where victims of identification theft in 2005. The latest statistical report shows that identification theft increased by 21%.

The Identification Act combats the challenges of Identification Theft, in the following ways. Firstly the Act strengthen the criminal laws governing identification theft 18 U.S.C. s1028, makes it a federal crime to:

---

[118] *Id.*

[119] *Id.*

Knowingly transfer, posses, or use without lawful authority, a means of identification of another person with the intent to commit, or to aid or abet and unlawful activity that constitutes a violation of federal law, or that constitutes a felony under any applicable state of local law. Secondly the Act focuses upon the victims. It has a centralized complaint hotline and consumer education service assist victims of identification theft[120].

The Identification Theft hotline has been in operation since 11/1/99. In July/August 2000, they received 1000 calls per week, 40% of those calls to the hotline where information request, of how to guard against Identification theft. The remaining 60% of the calls were victims of Identity Theft.

E.   The Computer Fraud and Abuse Act. 18 U.S.C. §1030

The Computer Fraud and Abuse Act was enacted in 1986. It protected computers against illegal cyber threats, computer trespass, damage, espionage from being corruptly used as a fraud instrument. It protected Federal computers, bank computer connected to the Internet directly affecting interstate and foreign commerce[121]. The act also includes provision to penalize the theft of property via computer, which is part of a defraud scheme. With the growth of computer related crime the Act was amended 8 times to includes the provision of Act below:

---

[120] Identity Theft and Assumption Deterrence Act. http://Spendonlife.com/guide (accessed June 6, 2011)

[121] Congressional research service (CFFA) 18 U.S.C. 1030 (e)(2) : Protected computers

computer trespassing (e.g. hacking) in a government computer, 18 U.S.C. 1030(a)(3)[122]

computer trespassing (e.g. hackers) resulting in exposure to certain government, credit, financial, or computer-housed information, 18 U.S.C.[123]

damaging a government computer, a bank computer, or a computer used in, or affecting, interstate or foreign commerce (e.g., a worm, computer virus, Trojan horse, a denial of service attack, and other forms of cyber attack, cyber crime, or cyber terrorism), 18 U.S.C. 1030(a)(5);[124]

committing fraud an integral part of which involves unauthorized access to a government computer, a bank computer, or a computer used in, or affecting, interstate or foreign commerce, 18 U.S.C. 1030(a)(4);[125]

threatening to damage a government computer, a bank computer, or a computer used in, or affecting, interstate or foreign commerce, 18 U.S.C. 1030(a)(6); and[126]

trafficking in passwords for a government computer, or when the trafficking affects interstate or foreign commerce, 18 U.S.C. 1030(a)(1).[127]

---

[122] *Id.*

[123] *Id.*

[124] *Id.*

[125] *Id.*

[126] *Id.*

[127] *Id.*

accessing a computer to commit espionage, 18 U.S.C. 1030(a)(1)[128]

Subsection 1030(b) makes it a crime to attempt or conspire to commit any of these offense. Subsection 1030(c) catalogs the penalties for committing them, penalties that range from imprisonment for not more than a year for simple cyberspace trespassing to a maximum of life imprisonment when death results from intentional computer damage. Subsection 1030(d) preserves the investigative authority of the Secret Service. Subsection (1030(f) disclaims any application to otherwise permissible law enforcement activities. Subsection 1030(g) creates a civil cause of action for victim of these crimes.[129]

VI. Proposed analyzed solutions and recommendations of privacy and safety when accessing the internet

In analyzing the problems of Cybercrime in Cyberspace, there is array of issues to debate. Cybercrime activity seems to be flourishing, with crimes being committed internationally against the U.S. and domestically by organized group of criminals who seem to winning the war of cybercrime. These organized groups of cyber criminal are set up exactly like a normal business organization. There target is the internet, and who much profit they can make from attacking it. Another issue at hand is the international aspect of cybercrime. There are various countries that don't do

---

[128] *Id.*

[129] *Id.*

enough to combat the problem. With the main reason being definition of cybercrime and what international laws if any that exist can punish the offender. It is extremely hard if not impossible for the U.S. to prosecute criminals who commit act of cybercrime internationally, due to jurisdictional issues and boundaries. This in turn causes a loophole in the justice of prosecution of international cybercriminals, allowing them to continue their organized activities of attacking computer through cyberspace.

Privacy is another issue to discuss; it is one of them main concerns of society today. Though there are laws in place, such as the Electronic Communications Privacy Act, protects consumer information from being accessed without their authorization. Many consumers are reluctant to make purchases on the internet in fear that their personal information will be fraudulently compromised. Victims of cybercrimes have suffered from Identity theft, loss of jobs, loss of income, etc… all due to their private allegedly protected personal information, which was inappropriately accessed, was used to commit unauthorized transaction. Computer victims spend countless months, sometimes years trying to correct the damage that has been done to their reputation and credit reports.

The struggle to solve the problems of cybercrime continues with no concrete way to stop it. The first line of prevention or remedy to cybercrime problems against consumers and businesses lies with user. At present online security measures that some web based companies offer do not protect consumer's personal information from being compromised.

According to March Rotenberg, Executive Director of the Electronic Privacy Information Center in Washington, D.C., states that the growth of e-commerce is hampered by the absence of consumer privacy protection.

The U.S. Federal Trade Commission functions to educate consumers and businesses about the importance of personal information privacy and accuracy of personal information when using the internet. The Federal Trade Commission also functions to protect consumer's privacy under the Privacy Protection Act, which reduces the effect of law enforcement search and seizure of personal documents, unless probable cause exists. The Federal Trade Commission guidelines guard against unfair and deception by enforcing companies privacy promises of how they collect, use and secure consumers personal information. The Federal Trade Commission believes that the lack of privacy regulation has led to looses in sales in the U.S. of 2.8 billion in 1999 and $18 billion in 2002. Federal Trade Commission former commissioner Pamela Jones Harbour[130] states companies must exercise responsibility before launching products on the internet, encryption must be used be Web based companies. Many providers chose not to use unsafe access SSL is used by default. A recent survey conducted by the National Center for education statistic show that 90% of school age children have access to computers either at home or at school, which in turn opens them up to privacy issues and concerns. There are various website that collect information of children

---

[130] Remarks Before Third Federal Trade Commision Exploring Privacy Roundtable. (Washington D.C.) http://www.ftc.gov. 3/17/10 (last viewed on June 6, 2011)

under 13 years old and they are required to comply with the Federal Trade Commission Children Online Privacy Act. With safety and privacy being a major concern when accessing the internet, consumer need not to rely on web based organization or government regulation and policies. Some which have proven to be ineffective in protecting consumers against cyber invasions. Web based companies, cyber hackers, internet child predators, etc., circumvent the safety tools that are in effect today.

There are certain measures a consumer can take to secure their personal information from being compromised when surfing the internet. Consumers need to be mindful of the fact that when accessing the internet, they are allowing information to be sent and received. There are security flaws in some of the major websites such as Amazon, Goggle, Twitter, etc. In my opinion they haven't done enough in securing there websites to prevent cyber attacks. When accessing the web via unsecured web site consumers need to be aware of the hidden dangers that exist. A poll taken by Wakefield Research and Wifi Alliance[131], reports that 32 % of computer access to a wireless network not owned by them, thereby putting themselves at risk for and cyber intrusion.

At issue is the capability to access information by the cybercriminal on a unsecured wireless network connection, offered at coffee shops, bookstores etc. There are numerous programs that are available and are being used by the cybercriminal for hacking identity theft purposes. These

---

[131] www.bbb.org/us/articln (last viewed on June 6, 2011)

programs are relatively easy to use for the purposes of obtaining personal information illegally from and internet connection.

The 5 most commonly used WiFi hacking software program used to commit cyber crimes are listed below:

1. Net Stumbler – is used to locate open wireless networks.
2. Kismet – Detects and displays the SSID's which are not being broadcasted.
3. Airsnot – Is an encryption security tool used to access encrypted connections.
4. Cowpatty – this tool will crack a network WPA-PSk protection.
5. Wireshark – Is used to shift through data flowing through the network.

These are some to the tools of the cyber trade which the cybercriminal uses to commit his/her cyber offenses.

The Federal Trade Commission recommends consumer need to be aware of this risk, especially at Wifi hotspots. They continue to states not to send personal information, private document, contact, etc, via and unsecured access. The following is the Federal Trade Commission recommendation when surfing a wireless connection[132]:

1. Make sure the connection is protected by a unique password.

---

[132] *Id.*

2. Transmitted information should be encrypted.
3. Don't stay permanently logged into a wireless hotspot.
4. Change your password frequently.

These recommendations should be adhered to, to prevent unauthorized access by cybercriminal when using a wireless unsecured connection.

1. Switch on the Web or Wap Encryption on the wireless router.
2. Change the default username and password set by the router's manufacture.
3. Turn on the firewall on the computer and router.
4. Avoid broadcasting your SSID.
5. Enable MAC based filtering.
6. Rename the default SSID.
7. Never auto-connect to a unsecured open network.
8. Static IP address are much safer.
9. Switch off wireless network if not using.
10. Place the wireless router in a safe place.

There are many other options that can help reduce the risk of your personal information from being compromised by unknown persons. Additionally I would suggest to consumers, to abide by the suggested safeguard measure, which can be taken to protect their personal information from being compromised when accessing the internet, or electronic communication from being accessed illegally.

1. Don't reveal personal information inadvertently. Properly configure your web browser to prevent the

dissemination of personal information without your knowledge.

2. Make up a password using cryptic letters or numbers.
3. Turn on cookie notices in your web browser. Allowing cookie control by blocking them from being sent to a third party.
4. Install a Virus protection program, which will protect your computer from worms and security threats.
5. Have multiple email accounts.
6. Never submit a credit card or other sensitive personal information without making sure the connection is secured.
7. Turn on email filter to send all received spam to your junk folder.
8. Read the website privacy guidelines.
9. Beware of websites that direct to a phony site, that request your personal information.
10. Use firewall protection which blocks communication from unknown sources.
11. Install Anti-Spy software to prevent computer threats such as Trojan horses, etc.
12. Maintain wireless security.
13. Avoid peer to peer sharing, which allows user's access to the entire computer file folders and sub-folders.
14. Turn off or disconnect your computer, which reduces malicious remote access to a Network.
15. Exercise the Opt out choices.

Upon a consumer being victimized by having his or her identification stolen, there are various recommended steps to take in order to attempt to undo the damage that is suffered from having your identity stolen. It is a time consuming process to repair identity, and can take up to two years to accomplish. By following the recommended outline, identity theft victims can start the process of correcting and protecting your personal private information from future harm[133]. Immediately contact the fraud department, of all 3 credit bureau's and request to place a flag or block on your credit profile and report. This will automatically flag your credit profile, additional clearance steps will need to be taken from creditors who make an offer or inquiry to your credit profile before approving a credit request or opening a new credit account in your name. You can also confirm or dispute any inaccurate or fraudulent debts on your profile caused by the identity thief. Request that the information be deleted or corrected, include in your correspondence that the debt derived from Identity theft and doesn't belong to you. Request your credit profiles form all 3 credit bureaus; review each credit report for accuracy. Contact any creditor of an account which have been tarnished or opened fraudulently. Be sure to follow up your correspondence appropriately if necessary with the credit fraud department. You may also need to submit an affidavit of fraud to the credit, describing date, amounts of the charges in question. Be sure to get it notarized. It is also recommended to close all compromised accounts and stop payment on any outstanding checks which may be fraudulent. Notify your bank to cancel checking and saving accounts, open new account with a new password and pin numbers. If your Social Security number has been used notify the Social Security office of the fraudulent act.

---

[133] James Walsh, Identity theft – How to protect your name, your credit and vital information, 2004.

Other place to notify:

1. Passport Office
2. Local telephone, electric, gas and water companies to warn them of a possible attempt to open a new account in your name.
3. File a complaint with your local Police Department of the theft.
4. If mail was stolen contact, the U.S. Postal Service
5. If your Driver License was used in the identity theft contact the Department of Motor Vehicle, to obtain a new license I.D. number.
6. Contact FTC to file an ID theft complaint.
7. Seek legal council if necessary if experiencing problems correcting fraudulent entries from creditors.
8. Contact your wireless carrier if the thief has established new phones in your name.

Updating and correcting errors on a credit profile will improve and correct your credit rating and score. It will also clear up the responsibilities for any debts that derived from the identify theft.

The level of security measure must be increased when accessing the internet via wireless, these and other security steps will reduce the risk of a cyber invasion. The level of security must also be taken by the website companies to make sure that while accessing their site wirelessly the user information will be secured. This will hopefully deter some of the efforts of the cybercriminal.

The outlook for cybercriminal to continues to be expanding. Though there are many laws in place to deter cybercriminal, they are still active in today's society. I myself have been targeted numerous times by cybercriminals. With all the self protected safeguards in place, cybercriminal still find a way to compromise personal information. As our reliance on computer continues, we need to be aware that there is other who are watching our ever key stroke, and the first opportunity they (cybercriminal) get's to invade your system they will. Education is the key to successfully combating cybercrime. Business organization should implement security cyber plans for deterrence from cyber attacks and incorporate and utilize informative resources to educate employee of legal consequences of breaching consumer confidentiality laws. Corporate guideline should be understood by every employee of an organization, the protection of sensitive data, records, software etc., is the forefront of the cybercrime issue.

Government infrastructure protection is another issue that needs improvement in fighting against cybercrime. One solution is to continue to create legislation that addresses the on wave of cybercrimes that are being created today. Prosecute and punish all offenders internationally and domestically. The U.S. government needs to step up their efforts in working with foreign countries concentrating on closing the gap of international cybercrime. International laws need to be universal, thereby removing the jurisdictional walls that prevent prosecution.